BIG HISTORY MAKERS

Remarkable Historical Characters Who Shaped Events–Explorers, Hawaiian Royalty, Adventurers, Missionaries

LaRue W. Piercy

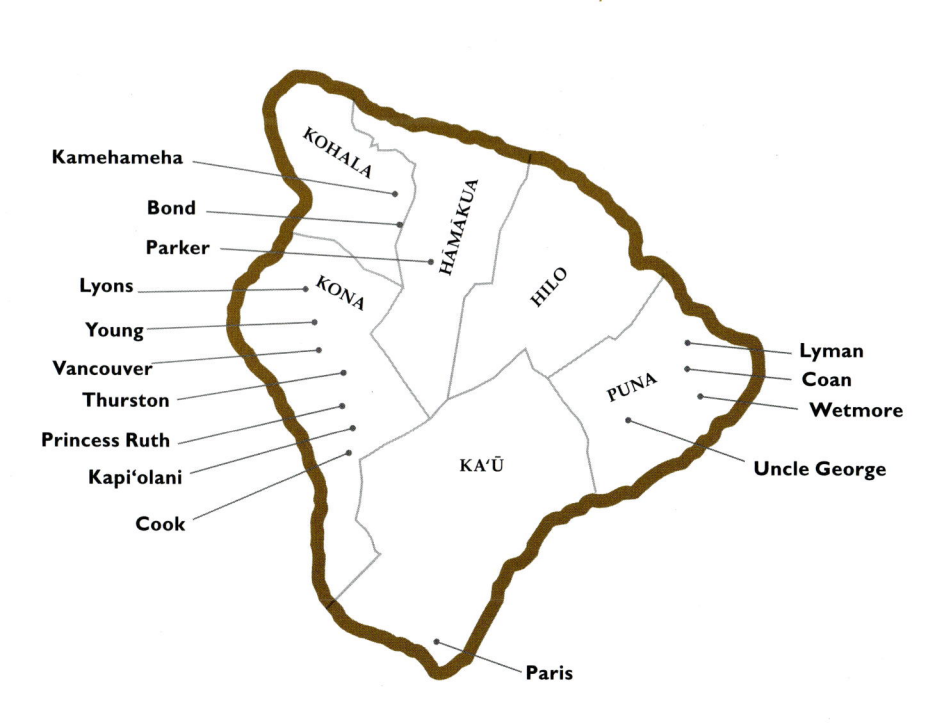

MUTUAL PUBLISHING

This is an edited reprint of *Hawai'i Island Leaders*
Copyright © 1990 by LaRue W. Piercy

All rights reserved. No part of this book may be reproduced in any form or by any electronic or mechanical means, including information storage and retrieval devices or systems, without prior written permission from the publisher, except that brief passages may be quoted for reviews.

Library of Congress Cataloging-in-Publication Data

Piercy, LaRue W.
  Big Island history makers : remarkable historical characters who shaped events : explorers, Hawaiian royalty, adventurers, missionaries / LaRue W. Piercy.
      p. cm.
  Includes bibliographical references.
  ISBN 1-56647-063-3 (softcover : alk. paper)
  1. Hawaii Island (Hawaii)--History--Anecdotes. 2. Hawaii Island (Hawaii)--Biography. I. Title.
DU628.H28P54 2007
996.9'10099--dc22
                                2007013043

ISBN-10: 1-56647-063-3
ISBN-13: 978-1-56647-063-6

Cover design by Leo Gonzalez
Cover illustration—Bishop Museum

New Edition First Printing, July 2007
1 2 3 4 5 6 7 8 9

Mutual Publishing, LLC
1215 Center Street, Suite 210
Honolulu, Hawai'i 96816
Ph: 808-732-1709 / Fax: 808-734-4094
email: info@mutualpublishing.com
www.mutualpublishing.com

Printed in Taiwan

TABLE OF CONTENTS

1	They Built the Hawaiian Kingdom	1
2	The Great Explorer Discovers Hawai'i	2
3	The King Who United the Islands	4
4	Two Englishmen Become High Chiefs	6
5	Sea Captains Come Bearing Gifts	8
6	The Unregenerate King	9
7	Saga of the Parker Dynasty	11
8	The Boy Who Sent the Missionaries	14
9	Those Poor Miserable Missionaries	15
10	Those Indomitable Thurstons	16
11	The Governor's Vices and Virtues	18
12	The Unhappy Life of Governor Ruth Ke'elikōlani	20
13	A Native Chiefess Serves God	22
14	They Started the Hilo Mission	23
15	The Lymans Lead the Way	24
16	Man of Great Talents	25
17	Doctor, Druggist, and Innovator	27
18	The Beloved Hymn Writer	28
19	No Task Too Hard for Brother Bond	30
20	He Built a Mission, Revived Another	32
21	Catholic Enterprisers	34
22	"Uncle George" Lycurgus Entertains	37
	Chronological List of Events	39
	Suggested Reading	42
	About the Author	43
	Other Big Island History Books from Mutual Publishing	44

A 1779 view by Weber of the waters off Kealakekua. *Hawai'i State Archives*

A sketch by Louis Choris of the Lanihau temple at Kailua-Kona. *Hawai'i State Archives*

1
THEY BUILT THE HAWAIIAN KINGDOM

According to the Polynesian legend of creation, the birth of the Big Island, also known as Hawai'i Island, was a blessed event of the gods, being the firstborn child of the god Wākea (sky or space) and Papa (the earth). But scientists, devoid of such spiritual fancy, assure us that the Big Island's actual birth from volcanic activity at the bottom of the Pacific came last in this chain of islands. It is still a youngster, less than a million years old.

The great mountain building outbursts started in the north, raising up the Kohala Mountains, then great Mauna Kea; mighty Mauna Loa's seemingly endless eruptions continued building the island. In time, soil formed, vegetation developed, and insect and bird life appeared and spread. And finally people came. Far ranging sailors of Polynesia braved the uncertainties and dangers of the powerful Pacific Ocean to seek a fresh life in new, unknown lands. They survived extreme hazards to reach the fresh, beautiful land of Hawai'i.

First, they came from the Marquesas Islands, northeast of Tahiti. So concludes Bishop Museum, judging from the types of bone fishhooks found in campsites at South Point. Radiocarbon dating indicates their arrival at 750 AD. By the year 1200 AD, the island was well populated by a new flow of immigrants from Tahiti and its nearby islands. From the Polynesian sacred island of Havaiki or Havai'i (Little Hava), now known as Raiatea, came the name Hawai'i, later applied to the entire island chain.

A legendary priest, Pā'ao arrived from Tahiti around 1000 AD, and built the Waha'ula Heiau at Puna and then the Mo'okini Heiau (now a registered national historic landmark) at 'Upolu Point in Kohala. 'Upolu was also a Polynesian island name from the South Seas homeland. Observing moral degeneration among the Hawai'i rulers, Pā'ao sailed back to Tahiti and brought back a king named Pili, who established a long line of rulers.

One descendent, Līloa, a sacred high chief, ruled his domain in Waipi'o Valley in the 15th century. His son 'Umi succeeded him, after routing his cruel and rapacious brother. 'Umi finally moved his court to Kona, henceforth the favorite residence of kings. After conquering the entire island, he built a temple between Mauna Loa and Hualālai and one at Kailua, whose stone slabs are now piled high in the corners of Moku'aikaua Church.

King Keawe, descendent of Pili, built the Hale-O-Keawe about 1550 AD, now reconstructed at the Pu'uhonua O Hōnaunau National Park, to preserve the bones of high chiefs.

2
THE GREAT EXPLORER DISCOVERS HAWAI'I

Captain James Cook,
Royal Navy
Hawai'i State Archives

Captain James Cook made the Hawaiian Islands known to the world by unexpectedly coming within sight of O'ahu and Kaua'i on January 18, 1778, and landing on Kaua'i two days later. He named them the Sandwich Islands in honor of the famed Earl of Sandwich, first lord of the British admiralty. He then sailed on his mission to look for the much sought Northwest Passage across America.

Cook was probably not the first foreign sailor to set eyes upon this distant land. It is likely that other foreigners landed on the islands accidentally in earlier times. Tradition records a Spanish ship wrecked off the South Kona coast between 1525 and 1530 AD. Only the captain and his sister escaped, married Hawaiians, and their families became prominent chiefs. Juan Gaetano, a Spanish navigator, may have rediscovered these islands in 1555.

Another story told by the missionary William Ellis, is of seven men landing on the Big Island in a painted boat, marrying native women, and becoming chiefs and good warriors. This matches the story of a boat from a Dutch ship landing on a Pacific island in 1699.

But it was Cook who explored the Hawaiian Islands and charted them. Returning from the American coast, Cook's two ships, the *Resolution* and the *Discovery*, spent eight weeks off the coast of Maui and the east coast of Hawai'i seeking a safe haven from the high seas, finally finding refuge in Kealakekua Bay on January 17, 1779. Welcoming crowds covered the shore and filled the bay when they arrived.

When Cook went ashore, priests ushered him to the Hikiau Heiau and performed an elaborate ceremony, decking him in sacred red kapa as their returning god Lono. The island king, Kalani'ōpu'u had visited the *Resolution* with other chiefs, including young Kamehameha during its stop in Maui. When the king returned to Hawai'i on January 25th, he paid his respects to Lono by visiting the ships.

The next day the king put on a grand formal welcoming ceremony as he and his chiefs, magnificent in their feather capes and helmets, with priests, idols, and food offerings, paraded around the ships in their fleet of double canoes. Going aboard Cook's ship, the king presented him with feather cloaks and gifts of hogs, sugar cane, coconuts, and breadfruit. Cook gave him a linen shirt, a sword, and other gifts later.

In spite of some minor incidents, all went well for the two and a half weeks before the ships sailed off north on February 4th. They got no farther than Kohala when the *Resolution*'s rotting foremast snapped in a violent storm, causing them to return to the bay and repair the severe damage on February 11th.

All went well at first, but on the unlucky 13th, trouble developed. A party of sailors who were getting water on shore were confronted by natives. A native on board the *Discovery* made off in his canoe with a pair of tongs and a chisel from the blacksmith's forge. Pursuers retrieved the stolen goods but got into a fight with a chief and some men when they attempted to seize the canoe. By the next morning, the *Discovery*'s large cutter had disappeared.

Cook's experience and policy in such cases was to seize the chief and hold him until his men returned the stolen property. So, the next day on February 14th, Cook took a boat to Ka'awaloa at the north side of the bay where Kalani'ōpu'u was staying.

As Cook, his lieutenant, and nine marines were heading back to the boat, the king's wife and several chiefs stepped in the way and begged the king not to go. He hesitated and sat down. A crowd collected, many armed with clubs, daggers, spears, and stones. Then came a report that Cook's guards at the entrance to the bay had shot a chief in a canoe.

Threatened by the angry Hawaiians, Cook wisely decided to withdraw his forces. When a native thrust a dagger at him, Cook fired a harmless shot from his gun. Then he fired again and killed a man. With that, the marines on the shore and the sailors in the boats began firing. Cook ordered them to stop, motioned for the boats to come in, and started towards them. The crowd exploded into action. A blow from a club felled Cook. As he tried to stand up, a dagger struck his back and sent him falling into the water. Either the blows had killed him or he drowned.

It took a week of occasional fighting and burning of some native houses before peace was restored and Captain Clerke, now in charge, could resume friendly relations with the chiefs. They returned some of Cook's bones and placed a kapu on the bay for Cook's funeral service on February 21st. The ships left the next day.

The first monument at the place where Cook died was an oak cross erected at Ka'awaloa by Lord Byron, commander of HMS *Blonde*, in 1825. Then in 1837 another British ship came to place a copper plate on a coconut tree near where Cook had fallen. The present monument was erected in 1874.

3
THE KING WHO UNITED THE ISLANDS

King Kamehameha
Hawai'i State Archives

"Kamehameha the Great" became Kamehameha's name after he united the Hawaiian Islands. Later he was referred to as the "Napoleon of the Pacific."

Kamehameha's parentage and date of birth both remain questionable. His unregistered arrival was probably between 1750 and 1760 AD. His accepted father was Keōua Kupuapāikalaninui, a stepson of Alapa'inui at whose Kailua court Keōua lived. Kamehameha's mother was Keku'iapoiwa, niece of King Kahekili of Maui the most powerful ruler of his day. Doubters of Keōua's fatherhood felt the lovely Keku'iapoiwa became pregnant when staying as a guest at Kahekili's court.

Warned by his priests that this child would become a man capable of overthrowing him, Alapa'inui was determined to destroy the infant. So friends of Keku'iapoiwa spirited her away to Hālawa in North Kohala. As soon as the baby was born, the runner Naole took him during the night and sped secretly away to Waipi'o Valley, where she brought up Pai'ea, as the boy was named at first, and protected him for five years.

By then, as Alapa'inui had grown old, it was safe to take the young boy to his mother at court. There he was named Kamehameha, the Lonely One, and received the tutelage proper of a growing chief. When Keōua, who succeeded Alapa'inui, suddenly became ill (some said poisoned), he had his brother Kalani'ōpu'u, the next king, train the boy. At court, Kamehameha proved himself a highly promising young chief.

Kalani'ōpu'u died in 1782, leaving his island kingdom to his son Kīwala'ō and allotting Ka'ū to another son, Keōua. To his nephew Kamehameha, he gave Waipi'o Valley and charge of the ancestral war god, Kūkā'ilimoku. This division of the island stirred up fresh jealousies and civil wars. Kīwala'ō decided to assert his rule over Kona and got Keōua to join him. The Kona chiefs chose Kamehameha as their leader and defeated the attackers at the battle of Mokuhai in the summer of 1782. Kīwala'ō was slain, but Keōua escaped to Ka'ū.

Kamehameha led two campaigns to win the island for himself; the second in 1785—both failed. In 1790, he successfully invaded Maui but had to give up a planned invasion of O'ahu when Keōua seized Hilo, killed his uncle, and then attacked Kamehameha's territories in Hāmākua and Kohala. After they battled to a draw, Keōua returned to Hilo. On his way back to Ka'ū, a terrific volcanic explosion killed 400 of his warriors, women, and children.

The following spring, in 1791, Kamehameha repulsed an invasion by Kahekili of Maui and Kā'eo of Kaua'i in a great sea battle marked by the use of cannons on both sides. This engagement interrupted a grand undertaking—Kamehameha's plan to build an immense heiau for his war god Kūkā'ilimoku on Pu'ukoholā near Kawaihae. Thousands including priests, chiefs, and commoners, joined in the great enterprise. After their leader's glorious victory, they resumed their work and completed the heiau that summer.

Later, two great chiefs went to Keōua and persuaded him to talk with Kamehameha at Kawaihae. As Keōua's great canoe approached the shore, there stood the imposing figure of Kamehameha in his regalia of feather cloak and helmet, ready to receive his royal guest. As Keōua prepared to step from the canoe, Ke'eaumoku hurled his spear and killed him, while others helped dispatch Keōua's companions in the double canoe. While Kamehameha may have been unaware of this plot, he profited by the elimination of his island opponent.

By 1794, Kamehameha was ready to strike out once more. He recaptured Maui and Moloka'i and then defeated O'ahu's forces, concluding his conquest in 1795 with a crushing victory at Nu'uanu Pali. With only Kaua'i left, he set sail a year later for his final island conquest, but strong winds and heavy seas swamped many of his canoes. He then had to return to Hawai'i to subdue a revolt in Ka'ū by Namakeha, brother of chief Kaiana, who after deserting Kamehameha was killed fighting him on O'ahu.

While Kamehameha ruled his kingdom from his native Hawai'i, he continued to build a fleet of canoes and schooners for an assault on Kaua'i. In 1804, while on O'ahu for a second conquest attempt, a serious epidemic severely crippled his army. He continued shipbuilding while cautiously conducting negotiations with Kaumuali'i, king of Kaua'i. In 1810, an American trader, Captain Nathan Winship persuaded Kaumuali'i to go with him to visit Kamehameha in Honolulu. There it was arranged that Kaumuali'i would still govern Kaua'i, but Kamehameha would be recognized as ruler of all the islands.

Satisfied, Kamehameha returned to Hawai'i and settled at Kailua in 1812 to enjoy fishing and farming. He took an increased interest in trading with the foreign ships that came to Kailua Bay. This he vigorously carried on until the spring of 1819, when he became ill; he died on May 8th. A trusted high chief secretly buried Kamehameha's bones in a cave that has never been discovered.

4
TWO ENGLISHMEN BECOME HIGH CHIEFS

John Young
Hawai'i State Archives

Isaac Davis and John Young

The villain of this tale is American trader Captain Simon Metcalfe, owner of two ships, the *Eleanora* and a small schooner named *Fair American*, which was commanded by his eighteen-year-old son Thomas. Included in the crew of the *Eleanora* were boatswains Isaac Davis, a Welshman, and John Young, an Englishman. By the time they reached India, they knew only too well of Metcalfe's penchant for cruelty, two officers having left the ship because of it.

Early in 1790, the *Eleanora* was anchored off Honualoa, Maui trading with natives. At night, some of the natives stole a small boat tied to the vessel's stern, killing a sailor in the process. Furious at this deed and unable to recover his property, Metcalfe fired on the village, killing several people. Later, learning that the culprits were from Olowalu, he sailed there, lured the natives to trade on one side of his ship, and then blasted the crowded bay with a cannon, causing a horrible slaughter known as the Olowalu Massacre.

Metcalfe engendered further personal animosity by striking with the knotted end of a rope a high chief visiting his ship during a stop on Hawai'i Island. The chief vowed vengeance against the next foreign ship. Fate brought the *Fair American* to the chief's district on the North Kona coast. The avenging high chief with four other chiefs and seven warriors went aboard to trade, but killed young Thomas Metcalf and his small crew. Davis, then serving on the *Fair American*, was wounded and jumped into a canoe, where he was mercilessly clubbed and left for dead. But he survived this ordeal and was taken ashore to Kamehameha. The king rebuked the high chief and retained Davis and the *Fair American*.

At that time, the *Eleanora* was at Kealakekua Bay. When Young went exploring on shore, he wandered too far to get back to the ship before it sailed. Natives could not help him because Kamehameha had put a kapu to prevent Metcalfe from learning the tragic fate of his schooner.

The next morning, natives took Young to Kamehameha. There he found his friend Davis, severely wounded and nearly blind. Metcalfe waited two more days for Young, then sailed. Retribution for his evil deeds caught up with Metcalfe four years later, when he and his crew were slaughtered by Haida warriors on the Queen Charlotte Islands near present-day British Columbia.

After an unsuccessful escape, Davis and Young settled down as assistants and advisors to Kamehameha. They helped conduct trade with foreigners and trained his men in the use of firearms. Their aid was important in the sea battle Kamehameha won against Maui forces and in later conflicts. The king rewarded them with grants of land and wives.

Davis owned lands on Hawai'i, Maui, Moloka'i, and O'ahu and served for a time as governor of O'ahu. Unfortunately he lost his life through court intrigue in April 1810. When King Kaumuali'i of Kaua'i was in Honolulu to make governing arrangements with Kamehameha, some chiefs plotted to kill the Kaua'i king. When Davis saved Kaumuali'i by revealing the plan, the plotters poisoned him. From his second marriage he had three children, who were adopted by Young. A grandson, Isaac Young Davis, became the second husband of Princess Ruth.

Young was called Olohana by Hawaiians from the "All hands!" command they heard him call out as a boatswain. As Kamehameha's representative, he managed the king's trade negotiations and took an active part in government during his forty-six years of life in Hawai'i. He served as governor of Hawai'i Island and other islands, and held landed estates on all five major islands. At Kawaihae, Young built his homestead, cook house, storage room, and a house for his children and their teachers. Parker Ranch later acquired 4,000 acres of Young's land.

Young had two sons, James and Robert, by his first wife, who died of cholera in 1804. Robert was sent to America for schooling, but was never heard from again after he was captured in the War of 1812. James successfully returned from a trip to England with Liholiho, Kamehameha II, who died of measles there. Later he visited America. He married one of Davis's daughters, Jane, and served as the governor of two islands.

Young's second wife, Ka'oana'eha, whom he called Mary Kuamo'o, was a niece of Kamehameha. They had four children. Their daughter Fanny became the mother of Emma, who would later be queen of Alexander Liholiho, Kamehameha IV. She was brought up by her Aunt Grace, wife of Dr. T.C.B. Rooke. John Young II, called Keoni Ana, was prime minister of Hawai'i from 1845 to 1854.

When the New England missionaries arrived in 1820, Young helped them to convince the king that they should be permitted to bring their religion to the islands. Missionaries often visited his home, a convenient stop at Kawaihae after crossing the channel from Maui.

In 1824, Young moved to O'ahu to live with his daughter Grace. He died on December 17, 1835, at age of ninety-three, and as a high chief of the kingdom, was buried in a marked grave behind the Royal Mausoleum.

5
SEA CAPTAINS COME BEARING GIFTS

Captain George Vancouver
Hawai'i State Archives

Captain George Vancouver visited Hawai'i five times, the first two times as a junior officer under Captain Cook in 1778 and 1779. Then he commanded official expeditions wintered in the Sandwich Islands in the early parts of 1792, 1793, and 1794. Vancouver understood the people, their leaders, and the warlike political situation. He aimed to prevent frictions and to better serve the interests of leading chiefs with whom be became well acquainted.

He recognized the superior abilities of Kamehameha and cultivated a friendly relationship with him, giving him much good advice. He expressed admiration for the king's "open cheerful, and sensible mind," believing to the end that Kamehameha was "of the most princely nature." But the captain was not about to arm the warring parties like so many traders were doing. Vancouver aimed to instill something other than combative motives in the chiefs' minds.

On Vancouver's advice, Kamehameha agreed on February 25, 1794, to cede the island of Hawai'i to the protection of Great Britain. But the British government never acted on this, though the British flag that Vancouver presented to Kamehameha flew over the royal headquarters for twenty-two years.

Considering the Hawaiian diet of fish and poi deficient in hearty sustenance, Vancouver magnanimously brought over cattle and sheep to fatten the people's larder and later delivered some goats and geese to replenish earlier supplies. Released on the plains of Waimea, the cattle eventually provided stock for Parker Ranch, having been allowed to run wild for ten years under a kapu prohibiting their being killed during that period.

This gift was not entirely fortuitous, since these rampaging, vegetation-devouring beasts upset the delicate ecology of the island's endemic plants and the habitats of indigenous birds; a problem still besetting the islands. The mighty koa forests could not be replenished because the seedlings had no chance to grow up into trees. Vancouver also distributed grapevines, orange and almond trees, and various garden seeds.

And Horses Keep Coming Too

In 1803, the American sea Captain Richard Cleveland, sailing the *Lelia Byrd*, figured on Vancouver's contributions by bringing horses to Hawai'i from Baja, California. Young at Kawaihae persuaded Cleveland to give him a mare and a foal, animals that aroused much astonishment and alarm when the natives beheld these odd creatures. Kamehameha, at first little impressed by horses, later became the first Hawaiian horseman.

By the 1820s, shiploads of horses were arriving from Spanish California, creating more of a wild animal problem; Hawaiians killed some, enjoying horse meat more than beef. Later, horses became the leading method of land travel and important to ranch development. They multiplied so quickly that a family might own as many as a dozen seedy-looking horses, and horse riders crowded the roads much like automobiles do now.

6
THE UNREGENERATE KING

Liholiho Kamehameha II
Hawai'i State Archives

On the death of Kamehameha the Great, his older son Liholiho, born to the highest ranking queen, Keōpūolani, succeeded the throne as Kamehameha II. He shared his rule with Ka'ahumanu, Kamehameha's favorite queen and Liholiho's guardian.

Hesitant to use his newly acquired authority, Liholiho finally yielded to the plans of Ka'ahumanu and Keōpūolani to break the power of the kapu and thus overthrow the native religion. Surprisingly he had in this decision the support of Hewahewa, the high priest.

Such a radical act stirred up revolt by a chief named Kekuaokalani and his followers at Ka'awaloa. An attempt at peacemaking failed. In a hard fought battle at Kuamo'o, on the makai side of the road that now connects Nāpō'opo'o and Hōnaunau, Kamehameha's forces fought to victory. Kekuaokalani and his wife (who had fought with him) were killed. A smaller rebellion at Hāmākua was soon quelled.

Another problem soon came with the arrival of the New England missionaries at Kailua. Liholiho was skeptical about a new religion, especially one that limited a man to a single wife and was against family intermarriage. Liholiho had five wives and his favorite was a half-sister. But he agreed to let the missionaries stay conditionally.

The king moved to Honolulu in November 1820. In July 1821, he sailed to Kaua'i, made friends with king Kaumuali'i, got him aboard his ship and carried him off to Honolulu. There Ka'ahumanu married him—and also married his handsome, almost seven-foot-tall son Keali'iahonui.

Though friendly with the missionaries and interested in their power of the printed word, Liholiho enjoyed his dissipations too much to be converted entirely to the restrictions of these demanding men of religion. In 1823, Hiram Bingham, leader of the religious band, tried to prevail upon Liholiho to "repent at once." The king confessed "my wickedness is very great," and did consent that "in five years, I will turn and forsake sin," though ignoring Bingham's warning that he was "not sure of five years, or five months, or five days."

Alas, how true! Liholiho and his favorite wife Kamāmalu sailed for England in November that same year and reached there the following May. After royal welcomes and entertainment, they succumbed to an attack of measles and died there in July. The frigate *Blonde*, commanded by Captain George Anson, and Lord Byron (a cousin of the poet) carried the bodies back to Hawai'i.

7
SAGA OF THE PARKER DYNASTY

John Palmer Parker (left), Col. Sam Parker (right)
Hawai'i State Archives

The great sprawling Parker Ranch in Kohala displays what the right man can do with initiative, industry, and honesty. It spreads over northern Hawai'i as an immense monument to its founder, John Palmer Parker. The Parker family saga is one of adventure and romance, resembling a lusty Texas soap opera.

The founding Parker, lured by Hawai'i's great attractions, deserted the New England trading ship that had brought him from his native Newton, Massachusetts, to the port of Kawaihae, Hawai'i in 1809. He was only nineteen years old and on his first voyage across the Pacific.

A friendly fellow, he soon had Hawaiian companions, a knowledge of the language, and a summons to the court of King Kamehameha, who admired his strength of character and put Parker in charge of the royal fish ponds at Hōnaunau.

But in 1811, Parker, now twenty-one, felt the pull of seafaring adventure once again and sailed off on another New England merchant ship to the Orient, only to be trapped in Canton harbor by the British during the War of 1812. That adventure persuaded him to remain in Hawai'i when his ship arrived in 1815. He was then twenty-five.

This time, Kamehameha, pleased that Parker had a musket and ammunition, appointed him to be one of the first men to kill the wild cattle. He was to supply tallow and hides for trade, and also sell salted beef, taro, and vegetable provisions to visiting ships. The king gave him a piece of land in Kohala near Pololū Valley. There he lived in a grass hut.

A year later, he won the love and the hand of a chiefess, a granddaughter of Kamehameha. He wed Kipikane in a traditional Hawaiian ceremony. At a Christian marriage after the missionaries came in 1820, she took the name Rachel Kipikane. Parker built a home at Maria, later replacing it with a frame house of koa. Their first child, Mary Ann Kaulalani was born in 1819, the year Kamehameha died.

After twenty years of breeding, the cattle had become so numerous and wild that they posed a threat. Parker shot them and captured some to form a herd. With the ever-increasing demand for beef, he found he needed experienced help. About 1830, Kamehameha III invited Mexican-Spanish cowboys to help slaughter and capture wild cattle and to train Hawaiians, who took with high spirits to this wild game. These cowboys were called paniolos, the Hawaiian word for Español. Of great assistance to Parker was Jack Purdy, who had also deserted his whaling ship at Kawaihae and who became as daring and efficient a cattle killer and roper as Parker. They also caught and trained some of the wild horses that Cleveland had brought.

Parker's first son, John Palmer Parker II, born in 1827, grew up thoroughly versed in his father's cattle business. He married a native girl named Hanai, of the bond slave class. The couple had a long and affectionate marriage, which produced only one child, Samuel, who died in infancy.

Ebenezer Parker

John Palmer Parker's second son, Ebenezer, blessed the original Parker home in 1829. Ebenezer grew into a handsome, wild fellow, enjoying the love of any woman he chose. Hearing of a girl of surpassing beauty on Maui, he sailed to Maui and found the girl seated in the yard of her grandfather's home. Seeing this handsome man standing transfixed by her loveliness, she invited him to come to her. It was a story book romance. Ebenener and Kilia fell in love as they talked and ate together. He proposed, but her grandfather opposed the marriage.

Kilia promised to go to Ebenezer when she planned to visit her parents in Hawai'i. Ebenezer returned home and watched the channel for weeks. Finally he saw her approaching with two canoes laden with her belongings. They married and lived together happily and faithfully. They had four children. Mary Ann Kaulalani II, Ebenezer II (who died at age ten), Samuel, and Nancy. Then tragedy struck. Ebenezer, only twenty-six, died from swallowing a sharp plover bone.

Kilia never recovered from the loss of her beloved partner. The Parkers took good care of her, helping her to raise her children, and John finally persuaded her to marry a Mr. King. She bore him two children. Six years after Ebenezer's death, while visiting Kohala, she yielded to a strong desire to revisit Maui, sailed off in her canoe, and amid raging seas, she and her crew were lost. She died on February 16, 1861.

Samuel Parker

John Palmer Parker's wife, Rachel Parker died the year before. Parker lived to age seventy-seven, dying on March 25, 1868. He divided the ranch between his son John and his grandson Samuel, with John serving as

Samuel's guardian until Samuel came of age. Inheriting the handsome looks of his father and the charm of his mother, Samuel was treated with royal lavishness by John and Hanai, with whom he spent vacations when not at school on Oʻahu.

Debonair Samuel led the gay life that his father enjoyed in his early days. But he lacked proper restraint with the renowned Hawaiian beauty Panana Napela whom he wished to marry. Her mother, incensed at her well-bred daughter's pregnancy, barred Samuel from communicating with her, told him that the child had died, and placed the baby girl with a relative, who after five years, gave her to an orphanage.

Panana was heartbroken. Samuel became desperate enough to return to his loved one's home and demand parental permission for their marriage. Panana's mother finally reconciled and conceded. Her uncle, a wealthy chief, gave the reunited couple a grand wedding and left his fortune to his favorite niece.

The Samuel Parkers led a royal life at Mānā and in Honolulu's high social circles with the Merry Monarch, King Kalākaua, who made Samuel a colonel. These were fabulous times for the family that included nine children, but not for the advancement of the ranch. As a well-respected political leader, Samuel devoted his administrative skills more to supporting Queen Liliʻuokalani and assisting in the transition to a territorial government than to running his ranch profitably. John Parker II, seeing his ranch deteriorating, declined mentally and physically and died on November 22, 1891. Samuel's son, John III, who had been legally adopted by his uncle John II, died at age nineteen on March 8, 1894.

Richard Palmer Smart

John's baby daughter Thelma inherited his half of the estate. The widow Elizabeth "Tootsie" Parker, Thelma's mother, in 1899 engaged Alfred Wellington Carter to serve as Thelma's guardian and as such manage the girl's half share of the ranch. Samuel then also offered his share to be so managed. Carter served wisely in making adjustments and improvements but at a high cost, which angered Samuel. A tough legal battle ensued. Samuel finally gave up and sold his half of the ranch for $600,000. The ranch now prospered. Carter saw that part of the profits went to benevolent and educational purposes.

Thelma grew up and married Henry Galliard Smart on July 25, 1912. Their son Richard Palmer Smart came along three and a half years later, the only one of the family to survive a fateful excursion to Paris. There, just before the war started in 1914, his mother gave birth to a daughter and both became dangerously ill, but they escaped Paris just in time. The baby died in New York followed by Thelma in San Francisco. Galliard succumbed to meningitis in November 1915, leaving Richard Smart sole owner of the great Parker Ranch. Smart died in 1992.

8

THE BOY WHO SENT THE MISSIONARIES

'Ōpūkaha'ia
(Henry Obookiah)
Hawaiian Mission Children's Society

'Ōpūkaha'ia, Henry Obookiah

After Kamehameha put down the revolt of Kaiana's forces in Ka'ū in 1802, a family of four fled to the mountains to escape death. They were pursued, finally captured and the parents were killed. Their ten-year-old son tried to run away with his baby brother on his back, but a spear ended the life of the little one and the boy was captured. His name was 'Ōpūkaha'ia, meaning "split belly."

He was kindly treated in his captor's home and later reunited with his uncle, who was the high priest at Hikiau Heiau at Kealakekua Bay. His uncle raised and trained him to become a kahuna like himself. Then, in 1808, the Yankee trading ship *Triumph* arrived in the bay. Naturally curious, Ōpūkaha'ia swam out to the ship, made friends with Captain Caleb Brintnall, and was invited to join his crew as a cabin boy and returned with him to America.

After an adventurous voyage to the Northwest coast, back to Hawai'i, to China, and then around the Cape of Good Hope to New York and New Haven, Ōpūkaha'ia, now called Henry Obookiah, found himself a rather lost soul in a strange land. A Yale student, Edwin W. Dwight, found Henry eager to learn and taught him to read and write, then arranged for him to live at the home of his father, Timothy Dwight, president of Yale College.

Fate seemed to favor Henry. At Yale he also met Samuel J. Mills, who became an inspired leader of the American missionary movement. It was Mills who helped Henry advance his education and religious interest as he worked for farm families in New England and lived with Mills at Andover Theological Seminary. It was Mills who induced the Congregational Church in 1810 to form the American Board of Commissioners for Foreign Missions, and later established the Foreign Mission School at Cornwall, Connecticut, to train foreign boys as missionaries to their homelands.

At school, Henry Obookiah was eagerly preparing to take the Christian religion back to his unenlightened countrymen. He was preparing a grammar for his native language and translating the Bible from its Hebrew text into Hawaiian, but he was not prepared to combat an attack of typhus fever. He died in a home at Cornwall on February 17, 1818, and lies buried in the town cemetery in a tomb that is engraved with the sad story of his short career. Many visitors at Moku'aikaua Church pause to read the reproduction of this brief legend, and at Kealakekua Bay they learn from a plaque that Henry Obookiah's "zeal for Christ and love for his people inspired the first American Board Mission to Hawai'i in 1820."

9

THOSE POOR MISERABLE MISSIONARIES

Publication of the "Memoirs of Henry Obookiah" stirred the hearts of those who knew him, and others who read of his sad eclipsed fate. The publication of the American Board's "memoirs" called for volunteers. Hiram Bingham and Asa Thurston, both graduates of Andover Theological Seminary, offered their services as ministers. Samuel Whitney and Samuel Ruggles were accepted as teachers. Elisha Loomis won a place as a printer. Thomas Holman filled the need for a physician. Daniel Chamberlain sold his fine farm, donated the proceeds to the board, and went off with his wife and five children to teach farming. The six bachelors scurried around to find willing consorts and all sailed from Boston on October 23, 1819, for Hawai'i.

After a long, wearisome, rough voyage on the trading ship *Thaddeus*, they reached Kailua on the Big Island on April 4, 1820. Here they had to win permission from Kamehameha II and his regent, Ka'ahumanu, to carry out their plans of educating and Christianizing the people. Young spoke favorably of their character and aims, but Liholiho was doubtful and delayed ten days before agreeing to allow a probationary year. The king requested that Dr. Holman stay, but the mission party picked the Thurstons to remain as missionaries. The rest, anxious and eager, sailed off to Honolulu on April 12th, leaving their four companions to huddle in a dirty hut and suffer in the hot sun in this arid land.

Their first night was miserable! The next morning, hot and flea bitten, they cleaned up their rough abode. Such rough conditions soon proved too much for the less adaptable Holmans. Lucia Holman deplored the "barren rocks," the rude heathenish people, the scarcity of water for washing, and the "heathenish" taste of the foods. The Holmans submitted to such unhappy conditions until July, when without mission approval they moved to the more attractive situation of Lāhainā, Maui. Later they were called to Honolulu, then to Kaua'i, and then back to Honolulu. Being rather independent characters and unable to adjust to missionary restrictions, they sailed back home on July 30, 1821. Quite the opposite in character and disposition, the Thurstons remained steadfastly at Kailua until November, when the king moved to Honolulu and the mission advised them to do the same.

10

THOSE INDOMITABLE THURSTONS

Asa and Lucy Thurston
Hawaiian Mission Children's Society

    The arrival of the second company of missionaries on April 27, 1825, gave the mission an opportunity to expand. Realizing that the Big Island should no longer be neglected, the mission sent Asa Thurston, along with two new men, Artemas Bishop and John Goodrich, as well as William Ellis, a visiting English missionary from Tahiti, to explore the island and to select the best places to start new stations. They left Honolulu, June 24, 1825, and returned on September 5th.
    The Thurstons then went back to Kailua with their two daughters, Persis born in 1821, and Lucy born in 1825. Bishop and his wife Elizabeth, a girlhood friend of Lucy's, accompanied them.
    In Kailua, Governor Kuakini built a church on a foundation of huge stones brought from a nearby temple that had been built by King 'Umi in the 15th century. The governor's men put up a thatched building sixty

feet long and thirty feet wide that seated six hundred to one thousand natives on floor mats. This building soon became inadequate for the twenty thousand Kona residents. Starting in February 1826, the helpful Hawaiians tore it down to replace it with a huge structure offering floor space for forty-eight hundred—"the largest and most elegant native building ever erected in Hawai'i."

For two years the Thurstons endured the uncomfortable conditions of their native village hut on the barren lava of the town. Then they built a large native house, a third of a mile further upland surrounded by protective walls. Later, they received a frame house from the mission.

On December 1, 1835, some malicious person burned down the magnificent native church. Builders went right into action, laying the cornerstone for the present church on January 1, 1836. The sturdy stone building was completed on January 31st of the following year and was dedicated on February 4, 1837.

The Thurstons had five children and were the only missionary couple to educate their children at home instead of on the homeland. In 1840, Lucy Thurston sailed back to America with four of her five children to place the older two, Persis and Lucy, in schools for higher education. Unhappily, her daughter Lucy died at New York City after the long voyage. Ten years later, Mrs. Thurston took the other children back. In all, she heroically made five long trips over the two great oceans.

Asa Thurston devoted nearly forty years to his mission and was much beloved by the people he served. He translated many books of the Bible "with purity and idiomatic accuracy." A series of paralyzing strokes forced Asa to give up his work at Kailua in 1861, when John Paris took over this church in addition to eight others in the Kealakekua area. Thurston died in Honolulu in 1868 at age eighty, forty-eight years after coming to Hawai'i. Mrs. Thurston who had survived a succession of sicknesses and hardships and a severe operation, lived until 1876, just sixteen days before her eighty-first birthday.

The Thurstons's daughter Persis married missionary Townsend Taylor and served with him at Lāhainā, Maui and in Honolulu. Son, Asa, married the daughter of missionary Lorrin Andrews. Their son, Lorrin Andrews Thurston, bought and managed the *Honolulu Advertiser* newspaper. His grandson, Thurston Twigg Smith, succeeded his uncle, Lorrin P. Thurston, who was a resident of Kailua-Kona until his death in 1984. The paper was sold to Gannett in 1993.

11
THE GOVERNOR'S VICES AND VIRTUES

Governor Kuakini
Hawai'i State Archives

John Adams Kuakini

This smart and capable man was governor of Hawai'i Island from 1820 to 1845 and acting governor of O'ahu from April 1831 to August 1833. He heaped many benefits on his missionary friends but not without causing them serious worries about his soul. He gave generous aid, built churches, and sought the honor of Christianity, but could not entirely give up his so-called "heathenish" ways.

Governor Kuakini, brother of Queen Ka'ahumanu and Ke'eaumoku (who was governor of Maui from 1820 to 1824), held high rank and was of exceptional intelligence. He preferred to be called John Adams, a name given to him as a boy. He was an independent soul bent on getting the best of two worlds, this one and the next, and not humble enough to attain the high standard of grace expected by Thurston and Bingham. Though he professed love to God, he found more pleasure and satisfaction in loving women and wealth. He was too human to yield entirely to the high Christian standards of behavior held by the missionaries.

He was a big, portly man, a "gigantic...native chieftain," as Bingham described him, supposedly weighing more than four hundred pounds. It is said that he had to turn sideways to get through the Moku'aikaua Church doorway. Admiring the advanced ideas brought by white men, he was eager to take advantage of opportunities to learn more. He readily took to reading and writing when the missionary press printed the first books in Hawaiian. William Ellis was impressed by his "desire after knowledge and improvement" and considered him handsome and dignified.

Christianity roused Adam's curiosity to know all about the Bible's mysterious things—the resurrection and destruction of heaven and earth at the final judgment, and just where are heaven and hell? And he inquired why, if most white men have read the Bible, do "such numbers of them swear, get intoxicated, and do many things prohibited by that book?" He made his own test of the powers of this new God. Before his brother's funeral, he slyly removed the body from the coffin "to see whether the foreign God would know the difference."

Though he failed to fit the Thurston standard of "no cavilling or questioning the truth of our doctrines," just accepting the truth of what "thus saith the Lord," the Thurstons lauded him for his support of "civilization, order, and improvement," his good laws, the schools he promoted, and the churches he had his people build. Lucy praised his reading and aid in translating the Bible, his prayers before eating, and his faithful church attendance.

Yet, with all that in his favor, he still could not win church membership. The missionaries believed that he still enjoyed his liquor, was unrepentant, and lacked a proper profession of faith. They shut the door in his face at the dedication of the church he provided in 1826. Though strict, Bingham admitted the mission's appreciation of "his kindness and cooperation," he declared that "They required something more than a readiness to read and hear the Word of God, to aid in building churches and in supporting schools, and to treat the foreign teachers with deference and kindness."

Later Bingham became encouraged that Adams "had come, at length, to admit the high claims of the Word of God," although the mission leader conceded the difficulty for such a man "confirmed in the love of sin, ever to break away, and feel deeply and right on the subject of personal religion." So Adams put on a good enough act to induce Bingham and Thurston to believe that he had changed "from a besotted skeptic" to a man "moral and devout." Such appearance of improvement won him church membership after a nine year struggle. While acting governor of O'ahu he waged a powerful war against alcohol and any boisterous fun making on the Sabbath.

He showed his power as a businessman, setting prices and not tolerating undercutting by the missionaries. In Hilo, he supervised the building of a church. He built a sawmill near Mauna Kea. When he learned of a missionary on Maui teaching girls to make cotton cloth, he had his wife and others taught to make cotton cloth too. He commanded his people to raise tobacco in spite of Thurston's prohibition of smoking. But the pleasure-loving Adams could not maintain his good Christian behavior. When a decade later, he married again to an eighteen-year-old girl from Hilo, Titus Coan declared "it is adultery of the most unblushing sort." Another act that by no means endeared him to the Congregationalists was his friendliness to the Catholic priests who came in 1840.

During his final illness, he refused to be converted by the priest who had served him well as a physician. He explained that each group had its own views on religion and he was willing to let it go at that. After he died in 1844 at the age of fifty-three, both missionary groups recognized the great good he did for them but had to acknowledge his "evil ways" also.

12
THE UNHAPPY LIFE OF GOVERNOR RUTH KEʻELIKŌLANI

Governor Ruth
Keʻelikōlani
Hawaiʻi State Archives

Though Hawaiʻi Island's governor from 1855 to 1869 Princess Ruth Keʻelikōlani, the great granddaughter of Kamehameha I is scarcely mentioned in history books. She had to battle reports that she was not the daughter of her father, Mataio Kekūanaōʻa, a governor of Oʻahu, and that the father of her mother, Pauahi, was not the son of Kamehameha. Though Ruth was not really a "princess," that title was later bestowed on her. Unlike others of her royal family, she clung passionately to her Hawaiian heritage and disdained foreign influence, especially that of the missionaries. She objected to being called "Ruth" instead of the Hawaiian form "Luka." She could speak English but refused to do so.

A six-foot-tall woman, weighing four hundred pounds, she became known as the fattest, ugliest, and richest woman in the islands. Her badly deformed nose, flattened by a botched operation, made her appear frightening to little children, though she loved them and could be a kind and gentle spirit. She was much loved by family and friends but often disliked by others.

After her mother died at Ruth's birth in 1826, Queen Kaʻahumanu served as her guardian until the queen's death in 1832. Ruth then went to live with her stepmother, Queen Regent Kīnaʻu, and with her half brothers, Moses, Alexander, and Lot, and her half sister Victoria Kamāmalu.

Ruth's marriage at sixteen years of age to young Leleiōhoku, Governor Kuakini's heir, proved to be a happy one, producing two sons, the second of whom died in infancy. But sadness was to be Ruth's lot. Her beloved husband died during the measles epidemic of 1848, having served as governor of Hawaiʻi, the position Ruth assumed seven years later. Ruth devoted herself to rearing her son, William Pitt Kīnaʻu, grooming him as a future monarch of Hawaiʻi. But tragedy struck again, when Kīnaʻu died in 1859 of an accident at age seventeen.

Ruth tried marriage again in 1856, taking as her mate Isaac Young Davis, a Waimea cattleman and grandson of Isaac Davis. The marriage was not happy. Resentful of having lost her first love, she and Isaac sometimes fought physically, especially after she, following a Hawaiian custom, gave their only child to Bernice and Charles Bishop. It was said that Ruth's operation resulting in her deformed nose was caused by a lusty blow from her husband. They separated after a year and Ruth finally divorced him eleven years later.

From her late husband Leleiōhoku, Ruth inherited vast properties, including Kuakini's stone mansion; though, firm in her Hawaiian ways, she preferred staying in a large native grass house on the property. This was torn down in 1884 and replaced by a two story frame guest house, demolished in 1927. Another grass house, on display to show visitors, deteriorated later and was removed. During her governorship, she moved to Hilo.

In 1835 she accepted the infant William Pitt Kalahoʻolewa, brother of Kalākaua, Liliʻuokalani, and Princess Likelike, renaming him after her lost husband Leleiōhoku and formally adopting him in 1862. He too was her pride and joy, growing up as a fine, well trained and educated youth, worthy of becoming a future king. But fate struck again, when he died of pneumonia in 1877 while attending school in San Mateo, California.

When Lot, Kamehameha V, died in 1872, Ruth, as his half sister, was one possible heir to the throne, as only she and Bernice Bishop remained in the Kamehameha line. Considered unfit for the position, Prince Lunalilo became the next king.

Perhaps Ruth's greatest claim to fame on the Big Island was her attempt to preserve Hilo from the raging river of lava threatening to destroy the town in 1881. Summoned from Honolulu by her admiring and faithful people, she took the steamer to Kona, made the hard, one hundred mile trip by wagon (in spite of her ponderous weight), and after sufficient rest to recover from her exhausting travel, placated

An 1880 group photo of Sam Parker (left), Princess Ruth (center), John Cummins (right). *Hawaiʻi State Archives*

Pele with propitious gifts of red handkerchiefs, liquor, and other donations uncorroborated.

Ruth's final feat was building an elaborate Victorian mansion in Honolulu, enough elegant to match that of Kalākaua's palace. She sold some of her lands to pay for the magnificent display. After two years' work, the grand house was completed in February 1883 and opened with lavish celebrations that also marked Ruth's fifty-seventh birthday. But such fancy living was not for Ruth. She slept on the lānai of her old home nearby.

Having taken ill the day after opening festivities, she returned to her grass hut in Kailua, where she died on May 24th. Her royal lands were inherited by the only other Kamehameha, her cousin Bernice Pauahi Bishop, who died on October 16th of the following year.

13

A NATIVE CHIEFESS SERVES GOD

Ka'awaloa, on the north shore of Kealakekua Bay, was the home of the high chiefs Nāihe and his wife Kapi'olani. Nāihe served as orator for the first three Kamehameha kings. Converted to Christian faith, Kapi'olani became eager to establish a mission and aid its progress at Ka'awaloa. Returning with the Thurstons to Kailua in 1823, the two chiefs held services in small villages, started schools, and built a small church at Ka'awaloa, which Asa Thurston dedicated on March 29, 1824.

So eager and determined was Kapi'olani to help the cause of the Lord, that she soon set out on foot across the island, enduring swollen feet, to give support to the struggling new Hilo mission. She also had a more courageous purpose: she would show the unconverted natives that Pele was no goddess, that the only living God was the one revealed by the missionaries. Descending to a ledge of the volcano crater on December 22, 1824, she defied the long worshiped Pele and proclaimed "Jehovah is my God." This deed won her acceptance as a bona fide member of the Christian faith at Ka'awaloa a year later.

Kapi'olani died in May 1841 from complications following a breast operation. She was highly respected for her outstanding efforts to further the missionary cause for nearly two decades. Her courageous action at the volcano won literary fame in a dramatic poem by Lord Alfred Tennyson.

14
THEY STARTED THE HILO MISSION

View of Hilo 1830
*Sketched by
Hiram Bingham*

Samuel Ruggles and Joseph Goodrich

No friendly welcome greeted the eager missionaries sent to remote Hilo in January 1824. Samuel and Nancy Ruggles, with three years experience on Kaua'i, and Joseph and Martha Goodrich, arrivals with the second company, had a rough beginning with people unfamiliar with white newcomers. But Kalanimōkū, prime minister, gave orders for the people to build a house and a church. The two isolated mission couples were still "suffering privations," by the time Kapi'olani arrived on her rescue mission about Christmastime that year, and encouraged the people to accept the mission values of education and reform.

By 1828, the work had progressed well enough that the Ruggles family moved to Ka'awaloa. The Reverend Ephraim Clark came for four months to bolster the lonely Goodriches and train teachers. Their wives were the first foreign ladies to visit the volcano. Governor Kuakini came to Hilo to direct the building of the church.

Goodrich was called away to Honolulu in 1826 and again in 1832 for two year periods, taking charge of the printing plant there, as he was a man of many capabilities. In Hilo, he raised sugar cane and made the first sugar and molasses there. He taught the people to raise coffee and other new food products. He was a good mechanic, made scientific observations, went fishing, and bullock hunting. He did so much other than preaching and teaching that Hiram Bingham was afraid that Goodrich was neglecting the Lord's cause. That situation plus the need of educating their growing family of five children prompted the Goodriches to return to the United States in 1836.

To fill in for Goodrich while he was in Honolulu (1831–1832), the mission sent Sheldon and Maria Dibble, who remained in Hilo until 1834, when they were transferred to Lāhaināluna. The Reverend Jonathan Green, with his wife Theodotia, also spent part of 1832 assisting the mission in Hilo.

15
THE LYMANS LEAD THE WAY

Sarah and David Lyman with four of their seven living children, about 1835
Hawaiian Mission Children's Society

David and Sarah Lyman became the real mainstays of the Hilo mission after their arrival with the fifth company in 1832. They devoted the rest of their lives struggling to build up and run the churches and schools in their district. Sarah faithfully filled her journal with the feelings and happenings in their lives during the next fifty-two years there. It took valiant spirits to overcome the problems of people, climate, and terrain, as well as the onslaughts of tidal waves, earthquakes, and threatening lava flows.

In 1834, the Scottish botanist David Douglas visited them, explored Mauna Kea and Mauna Loa, and left, planning to return in July. What arrived in Hilo was the body of the famous man. He had fallen into a trap for wild cattle on Mauna Kea and had been gored by a bull in the pit.

Sarah's busy record of the earthquakes, tidal waves, and eruptions proved helpful to scientists later— a severe earthquake in February 1834, a disastrous tidal wave in November 1837, a strong earthquake in January 1838, and stronger earthquakes on April 8, 1841, a tidal wave on May 17th, and then quiet until a Mauna Loa eruption flow threatened Hilo in late 1855 and early 1856. The worst earthquakes in the island's history came in the spring of 1868. Then Mauna Loa rampaged again from May 1880 to August 1881 to within a mere half mile of the Lyman home.

David Lyman's chief accomplishment was his creation and development of his Hilo Boarding School for Boys, the first truly manual training school. The boys gained worthwhile knowledge, not only from books, but also from manual work to develop vocational skills. The program, started in 1836 with the building of a schoolhouse and the enrollment of a dozen boys, provided a daily routine of prayers, meals, outdoor work, classes, recreation, and study. The school became an incentive for other such schools in the islands and later in America.

In 1839, needing larger quarters, David built a new schoolhouse, dormitory, cookhouse, and even an infirmary for isolation of contagious diseases. The first attack of measles hit all fifty of their boys in 1848, but David administered to them, while Sarah took care of the family, and not one succumbed to the disease which took a tenth of the island population. The Lymans also built a new house with a large steep thatched roof with two dormer windows. This house, enlarged in 1856, now stands as a museum of early missionary life.

The king granted the school forty acres of land in 1849, providing greater agricultural training and a supply of food for the school. Then a maliciously set fire burned down the schoolhouse in 1853. A temporary thatch structure provided classrooms until a worthy replacement could be built three years later, with five hundred dollars funded locally and four thousand dollars from the state legislature.

Such continual problems and labors left the couple nearly exhausted in later life. After two years of failing health, David died on October 4, 1884, at eighty-one. Sarah lived fourteen more months to age eighty, passing away on December 7, 1885.

16

MAN OF GREAT TALENTS

Fidelia and Titus Coan
Hawaiian Mission Children's Society

The most spectacular organizer, evangelist, and influence on missionary endeavors in the islands was Titus Coan. He and his faithful wife Fidelia, members of the seventh company, proved a godsend to the weary Lymans in 1835.

Titus proved himself a man of vast energy, physically, mentally, and spiritually. The accounts of his quarterly travels to visit churches and schools in the district are tales of daring, in getting across torrents raging through precipitous channels. As a scientific observer, he risked his life to climb Mauna Loa to gain close-up views of fiercely cascading lava flows. But his great missionary talent was that of keeping in close touch with all his people, collectively and individually, and preaching to them with wholehearted conviction.

On his visiting tours, he examined schools and served as a doctor as best as he could, keeping a record of each person and checking up on each one on the following visit. Such visits became an important event in their lives, for he knew them all by name, counseled them, and helped them. They loved him. He also handled cases of discipline, admonishing those who had committed sins.

His powerful preaching served to draw people to Hilo, increasing its population to some ten thousand. His willing followers voluntarily hauled to town great quantities of timber to build a church so vast it could hold as many as five thousand. Coan's great "day of days" came on July 7, 1838, when he dramatically baptized 1,705 specially selected from his list of three thousand. In the year May 1838 to May 1839, the church took in 5,244 members.

In 1840, a mighty wind destroyed the great native church. Coan supervised the building of a new one, entering heartily into the heavy work of hauling down trees. This well-built frame building, dedicated on June 1842, also gave way to age and dilapidation, so on November 14, 1857, the people laid the cornerstone of the present Haili Church, dedicated on April 8, 1859.

It was Coan who originated the plan of having American school children donate ten cents to pay for a ship to provide extended missions to the Marquesas Islands and Micronesia. When the *Morning Star* came into operation, Coan sailed on it to the Marquesas Islands in 1860 and 1867. In 1870, he and Fidelia, who needed medical attention, traveled to the eastern United States, where he became a prominent figure addressing meetings, conventions, and churches, and visiting universities.

Nevertheless, the trip failed to help restore Fidelia's health and she died on September 29, 1872, at the age of sixty-two. Hers was the first grave in Prospect Hill cemetery. Titus carried on for ten more years until December 1, 1882, the year his autobiography was published.

17
DOCTOR, DRUGGIST, AND INNOVATOR

Charles and Lucy Wetmore
Hawaiian Mission Children's Society

Arriving with his wife Lucy in 1849, a year after the twelfth and last mission company, Charles Wetmore was sent to Hilo to provide the island with its own physician once again, and Hilo with its first druggist.

His early start of vaccinations prevented the 1853 smallpox epidemic, sparing the Hilo population. He proved to be a good businessman, charging fees for those outside the mission he served. After the Mission Board in 1855 discontinued its support in Hawai'i, he found it profitable to dispense drugs to visiting ships and built his first drug store on the beach the next year. At the same time he faithfully kept up his medical practice.

When their son Charles, devoted to taking up his father's career, died at age fourteen after an active summer serving as a cowboy at a ranch, his sister Fannie pledged to become a doctor. She returned from her American training in 1882 to become a much-loved addition to the Wetmore medical services. While his daughter was away, Charles rigged up the first telephone line on the island in July 1879.

An ingenious man, Charles installed a big bathtub in their house, conveniently filled with cooling waters from the brook near their house. This provided a refreshing hot-weather luxury. But it also spelled tragedy. On a torrid day in July 1883, the doctor came home to find his dear wife Lucy drowned in the tub, having evidently hit her head and sunk into the water unconscious. The doctor continued his duties with the expert aid of his daughter until he passed away on his seventy-eighth birthday on February 8, 1898.

18
THE BELOVED HYMN WRITER

Lorenzo Lyons
Hawaiian Mission Children's Society

Lorenzo Lyons

When lovely little Betsey Lyons and her diminutive husband Lorenzo stepped ashore in Hawai'i, the natives exclaimed, "Why, the very children are coming to teach us." They became the best loved of the missionaries.

Sent to Waimea in July 1832 to aid the Baldwins, Lorenzo valiantly tackled the job, traveling up and down forty miles to Kohala and then to Hāmākua, taking five or six weeks to complete his tours. A sensitive, sympathetic soul, he lamented the wretched conditions of the people and strove to help them in every way he could.

Betsey was elated to find her sister Emily arrive in April 1837 with the eighth company as the wife of Isaac Bliss. With Lorenzo, she hurried to Honolulu for a happy reunion on April 29th. A week later, Betsey became ill. Her condition quickly grew worse, culminating in her death on May 14th. Lorenzo was heartbroken. Their devotion had been deep and true.

By July 19th, he was back in Waimea preaching and teaching. Lorenzo devoted himself to teaching twenty-five hundred children and about as many adults in his schools. He took care of the sick during an epidemic of mumps. And, like Titus Coan, he preached so convincingly that he garnered almost twenty-nine hundred converts. He earnestly promoted better housing, agriculture, and the spirit of helpful neighborliness. He was one with the Hawaiians, both in thought and in speech.

With such heavy burdens as well as one surviving son to care for, Lorenzo, still mourning the loss of his dear Betsey, made his way to Hilo and there he married Lucia Smith on July 14, 1838, who had also come with the eighth company as a single woman. She proved herself an efficient helpmate and loving mother to his son, and also mothered three children of her own. Later in life, as Lorenzo wore himself out with his never-ending tasks, she took over more of the physical work, started a school for girls, and outlived her husband by five years, dying in April 1892.

Lorenzo meanwhile labored on, following his personal philosophy, "Let the body and mind be constantly active." He made the rounds of his district, working his way over twenty or thirty precipices to come home exhausted. In 1848, he too had to cope with the measles epidemic, and then attacks of diarrhea, dysentery, and whooping cough. The next year he almost drowned while trying to land in a canoe at Waipi'o. A terrific thunderstorm in 1850 flooded homes and a meeting house. Then came the smallpox epidemic in 1853.

In 1855, heavy storms again battered the church so fiercely that it had to be abandoned and a new one built. The cornerstone was laid on August 29th and the present 'Imiola Church was dedicated in 1857. Lorenzo also built fourteen small churches in other parts from 1860 to 1867, but by 1863 he was too worn out to continue making the district tours he enjoyed so much and had to leave these other areas to native preachers he had trained.

On July 16, 1872, the people joyously celebrated the fortieth anniversary of Lorenzo's arrival. He was then serving as postmaster and school agent. His jubilee celebration ten years later was more subdued, as he confessed himself to be too feeble. But gifts from all corners of the island poured into the mission house. He was proud of being the first missionary in Hawai'i to complete fifty years of continuous service.

Hymn writing was one of Lorenzo's great contributions to the spirit of Hawai'i. He considered himself a poet laureate as he turned out volumes of hymns with great poetic purity. He lived Hawaiian in spirit, talked pure Hawaiian, and even thought in Hawaiian. His great spirit lives in the hymns, especially *Hawai'i Aloha* which people today stand to sing with reverence.

Worn out with his devoted labors, Lorenzo passed away on October 6, 1886. The family burials near the Lyons's home were moved to the pre-sent site near 'Imiola Church, and are marked by a white marble shaft, next to the old church bell.

The children of Lorenzo Lyons—Elizabeth (left), Albert (center), Fidelia (right). *Hawai'i State Archives*

19
NO TASK TOO HARD FOR BROTHER BOND

Elias Bond about 1855
Hawaiian Mission Children's Society

To replace the misfit Isaac Bliss, the mission appointed Elias Bond. But Bliss returned to Kohala and acted so erratically that Bond complained to the mission. Fortunately, Bliss left, and Bond energetically took over this difficult territory. Like Coan, he made four tours each year and kept personal records of each church member. Bond became such an important figure there that King Kamehameha IV referred to him as "King of Kohala."

Bond also developed a new type of school for training native teachers, a forerunner of normal schools in America. He made blackboards for his classrooms. His schools became the best in the islands. He also provided a boarding school for select boys in 1842 and kept it going until 1878, when it became a government school. After further instruction in Hilo, many students returned to become teachers.

Constructing a substantial church building was one of Bond's greatest problems. He got rid of the first tumble-down, flea-infested, thatch structure. The congregation worshipped in a new sugar mill while building another thatched church, which soon suffered due to high winds and heavy rains. In 1848, Bond and his faithful followers began assembling materials for a really strong church. Bond exerted all his physical forces in directing the prodigious task of cutting trees and dragging them over precipitous banks ten or fifteen miles, often in drenching rains. A series of problems delayed construction before the building was completed three years later. After all this tremendous labor, Bond and his people only benefited for four years. In December 1849, a terrific gale demolished the new church.

Bond and his followers again gathered materials, but this time for a strong stone structure. They started building in 1853 and finished in October 1855, presently Kalāhikiola Church.

Bond was the first missionary to renounce support from the Mission Board and go off by himself, receiving a small salary from his congregation. Offered greater financial rewards in other fields, Bond steadfastly clung to his "first love," Kohala. Seeking to provide work and income for his people, who were rapidly drifting away to more remunerative fields, Bond organized the Kohala Sugar Company in February 1863 and directed it with his customary devotion and energy until it became a profitable business nine years later.

Though this undertaking was enough to wear out any man, Bond still struggled with widespread missionary problems. For fellow white men working at the sugar mill, he started church services in English in 1865 and dedicated a new house of worship in 1869. By then, his mind became so strained, he almost gave up. He preached at Kalāhikiola but turned the smaller churches over to his trained assistants.

Having long dreamed of starting a girl's school, with funds from outside sources, Bond opened a school in December 1874, after working hard himself in its construction. Lorenzo Lyons's daughter Elizabeth served as principal of Kohala Seminary. A separate schoolhouse was added in 1878. Facing a typhoid epidemic, getting proper teachers, and Elizabeth's retirement in 1882, the school closed in October that year. It reopened in 1889 under the management of the Hawaiian Evangelical Association until 1926, then it was used until 1956 as a boarding home for Kohala High School students.

A true scholar and authority on correct Hawaiian usage, Bond could give spellbinding sermons two and a half hours long and completed a fourth revision of the Hawaiian New Testament in 1880. Like Lyons, he also served as postmaster, until 1880.

In her own sphere, Ellen Bond, Elias's wife, too was devoted to her mission and family labors, raising nine healthy children born between 1841 and 1859. A tenth one died in 1861. After forty years of such faithful service, she passed away on May 12, 1881, and was buried under the trees in the garden.

Her loss sapped Elias's ambitions for a time, but he soon returned to his routine, making his one hundred sixtieth quarterly tour of churches and schools. The dividends he received from the sugar plantation were distributed to the American and Hawaiian boards as well as to schools and colleges, and foreign missions. In 1890 his alma mater, Bowdoin College in Maine, awarded him the degree of Doctor of Divinity.

He officiated at his local church until his seventy-first birthday, August 19, 1884. In January 1885, he was succeeded by a former pupil, the Reverend S. W. Kekuewa. From then on, he suffered, crippled and in pain for twelve years, helpless for almost five, until he died on July 24, 1896, at eighty-three having given fifty-five years to the people of Kohala.

20
HE BUILT A MISSION, REVIVED ANOTHER

John and Mary Carpenter Paris with Ella and John Jr. about 1855
Hawaiian Mission Children's Society

John Paris Opens Waiohinu Mission

One more mission was needed for Ka'ū, between Hilo and Ka'awaloa. That assignment went to John Paris, who with his wife Mary Grant arrived in the ninth company in May 1841. After the birth of their daughter at Honolulu in August, the Parises sailed to Ka'awaloa, where Mary stayed while John and Cochran Forbes, an English carpenter, sailed down to Ka'ū to prepare a native house for the furniture Paris had brought in a canoe.

Back at Ka'awaloa, John loaded his wife, baby, and belongings into a canoe and sailed back to Ka'ū. Then, by wearisome trek, they made their way up to their small, crowded little home, which had to make do for the first six months. Heavy gales assailed them for weeks.

John Paris knew how to get things done. He had the carpenter build a stone kitchen house in which they lived until the natives, with John's expert direction and help, could complete a large thatch house. Two years later, John was provided a more roomy and comfortable frame house of koa wood, dragged by natives from the forest fifteen to twenty miles away. This beautiful koa wood was the "cheapest" they could get then.

The Parises became good friends with the Coans in Hilo, for Titus had formerly worked in the Ka'ū district. On a visit to Hilo in January 1843, John joined Titus on one of his climbs up the erupting Mauna Loa, a reckless experience that almost cost them their lives. They returned only after "three days of hobbling on lame feet."

Paris started preaching in a common native meeting house; in time, his congregation built a stone structure mortared with coral and with a thatched roof. Paris's faithful congregation hauled heavy stones from Hawaiian temples in the district, corals from miles out in the sea, and timbers from the forests of Mauna Loa. This building served as their church until the great earthquakes of 1868, and was replaced later by the present attractive frame structure.

Mary Paris succumbed to a serious illness. The doctor was summoned to her aid but could not help her, neither could the doctors in Hilo or Honolulu. She died at the Coan home on February 18, 1847. Fidelia took care of the two young Paris daughters while John returned to carry on his work for two more years.

Others Carry On

The eleventh company that arrived at Honolulu on July 15, 1884, brought Timothy Dwight Hunt and his wife Mary, who were sent to Wai'ōhinu to help Paris. They stayed just a year. Then Henry and Maria Kinney of the twelfth company joined Paris in 1848. They took over the mission when Paris left to return to America in 1849. Illness forced Henry's departure in 1854, and his death that same year.

William and Jane Shipman succeeded the Kinneys, but Shipman too died at Punalu'u, Hawai'i on December 21, 1861. In 1862, Orramel Gulick, born in 1830 to Peter and Fanny Gulick, missionaries with the third company in 1828, came to Wai'ōhinu with his wife Ann Clark, a missionary daughter, and remained until 1865. Then came the Pogues in 1866, who served at Ka'awaloa from 1848 to 1850. They stayed for two years, and were the last of the missionaries assigned there.

Restoring Ka'awaloa Mission

After the Pogues left the Ka'awaloa station in 1850, it remained vacant until the return of John Paris in 1852 with his new wife Mary Carpenter, whom he had married in Boston, September 7, 1851.

As a refuge from the hot, humid climate of the shoreline, Ruggles and Forbes kept a grass cottage at higher elevation on Kealakekua. Paris, a capable builder, first built a stone kitchen and lived there while he built a good wooden house. To save his single horse for journeys through his district, he walked "up and down the steep, hot, rocky trail" to the church below.

Since the grand new stone church lay neglected for so long, the only remedy was for Paris to rebuild it. For the declining population, he put up a smaller but well built church in three years, and named it Kahikolu or Trinity Church. This is the present building, as renovated in 1984.

Paris also had to rebuild churches and schoolhouses in his district and revitalize the mission's work. He set up seven other small churches, trained native pastors, added the Moku'aikaua Church when Asa Thurston had to leave it in 1861, and labored to keep nine churches active.

He continued his work in the district throughout his life, except for the period from 1870 to 1874, when he was in Honolulu to develop a theological seminary, and another year there in 1880. After that, he returned and built a new house and carried on his church work, visiting the sick and unfortunate, and counseling native pastors. He died in 1892 and his wife four years after him.

21
CATHOLIC ENTERPRISERS

"Baptism aboard the *L'Uranie*," an engraving from an original drawing by Jacques Arago shows the baptism of Kalanimōkū on August 14, 1819. It was the first Christian ceremony in the islands.
Hawai'i State Archives

Father Robert A. Walsh and Louis E. Heurtel

A year before the arrival of the Congregationalists on the *Thaddeus*, the Hawaiian high chief Kalanimōkū ("prime minister" to Kamehameha and thus called "Billy Pitt" after the then British prime minister), at his own request, received a Catholic baptism aboard the French ship *L'Uranie* in 1819. Catholic priests were opposed by the Protestant missionaries and were refused entrance by the Hawaiian government until 1839, when the French government sent a frigate to Honolulu to demand equal treatment for all Christian denominations.

Father Robert A. Walsh, in Hawai'i since 1836, arrived on Hawai'i Island June 26, 1840 with Father Louis E. Heurtel, a recent arrival. From Governor Kuakini they obtained the land where Saint Michael's Church in Kailua now stands and put up a small chapel. Kuakini also granted them Queen Ka'ahumanu's house, just south of Moku'aikaua Church, as living quarters. The stone hitching post that once stood in front of the house now rests inside the Kona Plaza Arcade.

After the two priests had six hundred fifty-five converts in Kailua by the close of 1841, Father Walsh set up a mission at Waimea with Father Denis Maudet in charge, and traveled to Hilo and Puna, and returned to Honolulu. Three other priests joined the missions on Hawai'i—Father Stanilas Lebret at Kohala, Father Joachim Marechal at Ka'ū and, Puna and Father Pouzot at Hilo.

Father Heurtel remained in charge of the island priests and of the North and South Kona missions. His good medical training gave welcome aid to many ailing Hawaiians. He became a friend of Kuakini after curing him when the Protestant doctor failed. Like the Protestant missionaries, he and other priests on the island experienced extreme difficulties in reaching outposts all around the island, traveling by canoe or by foot over rough lava, or up and down deep gulches often drenched by rain, or almost overcome by the hot sun.

Catholic progress was slow in Kailua, where the Protestant chiefs and their people dutifully regarded the newcomers as Palani (French) and papists. The priests did find a friendlier welcome at Kaloko, north of Kailua, where they built up a loyal nucleus of converts. The priest then got the governor to build a larger church at Kailua for eight hundred dollars, but the construction was so poorly done that Kuakini settled for six hundred dollars. In 1842, a school for children was added.

Father Joachim Marechal

That same year Father Heurtel sent the energetic Father Marechal to Ka'ū, where he was confronted by strong Protestant opposition. Father Heurtel advised him to "proceed with prudence, charity, and patience toward all enemies." Father Marechal gained the friendship of the high chief and got written approval from Kuakini. With vigor and the growing enthusiastic support of his converts, he spread his influence to all seventy little villages in Ka'ū. He endured heavy hardships, wearing out shoes and cutting his feet as he trudged over rough, sharp lava fields to build chapels and schoolhouses, and counsel his people. By 1846, he had converted two-thirds of the population in Ka'ū.

In 1847, he was called back to Kailua to replace Father Heurtel, who was worn out from his long and difficult travels back and forth to Kohala and to Ka'ū, and was transferred to Tahiti. By May 1848, Father Marechal became a superior of the mission and took charge of all of Kona. With three new priests to aid him, he had Father Agathange Grould take over his former district of Ka'ū, Father Gregory Archambault replace the transferred Father Lebret in Kohala, and Father Eustache Prestseille to work in Puna.

Continuing his untiring efforts, Father Marechal set about building the present Saint Michael's Church in Kailua, dedicated in 1855. But he too was wearing out. He held his last baptism on Christmas 1858. Two priests came to aid him until he died on April 21, 1859, at the age of forty-five, after nineteen years of struggling valiantly against the island's severe difficulties.

Catholic churches spread in the Kona district as a result of the efforts of these early priests. At Hōlualoa, the Immaculate Conception Church is the district parish church with the district priest in residence. By the sea at Kahalu'u rests the most photographed mission chapel in the state, charming little Saint Peter's.

The Painted Church

The much viewed Saint Benedict's, famed as the "Painted Church," developed from the small Saint Regis Chapel by the sea at Nāpō'opo'o. For two years, a fresh, young priest from Belgium, Father Lorteau served there and was greatly loved by the Hawaiians. Exhausted by his duties during an attack of influenza in 1898, he was taken aboard a ship sailing to Honolulu but died en route.

Another Belgian priest took his place: Father John Berchmans Velghe. As most people then were living two miles higher to enjoy cooler climes and more fertile soils, Father Velghe moved what he could of the chapel up to its present location and dedicated it to Saint Benedict in 1902. A veteran of missionary work in the Marqueses and with a love of painting, he decided to attract his people with colorful pictures of biblical scenes on the inner walls of his church. But he too became worn out with his labors and had to return to Belgium six years later.

Other Priests

While Father Eugene Oehmen was in charge of South Kona, three lava flows from Mauna Loa spilled down in 1916, 1919, and 1925. The last one hit the lower villages, rushing across the highway and into the ocean. Above the highway where the town of Hoʻōpūloa and Saint Peter's Chapel stood, an obelisk of rock holding a simple iron cross now marks the spot. A new village and church were built at Miloliʻi.

In Kohala, Father Lebret worked (except for three years in California, from 1841 to 1876) zealously to cover the area, including Hāmākua. Nearly blind, he died in Honolulu in 1878 at age seventy-nine.

Two young priests came to the island in 1864. Father Clement Evard assigned to Kohala, found the work and hard travels too wearing. So the bishop reassigned him to Puna, bringing the other stronger and more energetic young priest, Father Damien DeVeuster to Kohala. Father Damien vigorously carried on the work in Kohala and Hāmākua from 1865 to 1873, until his request to go the leper colony on Molokaʻi was granted.

Father Charles Pouzot

It wasn't until 1846 that Hilo had its first regular priest with the arrival of Father Charles Pouzot. Young Henry Lyman, son of the Protestant missionary, records how terrified he was at the sight of such a dreadful being as a Catholic priest. But as he grew, he found a good friend in this "saintly seeming personage" and enjoyed French lessons with him. Lyman recorded that the priest welcomed into his three grass thatched chapels those "hardened sinners" who smoked and drank and whom Titus Coan expelled from his righteously minded flock.

The kind priest prepared a larger, less fragile frame chapel in 1848, dedicating it to Saint Martin. Sympathetic sailors aboard an American warship at Hilo that July donated a bell and money. And Catholic sailors from another American warship in 1852 took up a generous collection to help enlarge Saint Martin's. Six years later, that building was again too small for the growing congregation. The congregation raised money to build a new church, Saint Joseph's Church, completed in July 1862.

Father Pouzot also had charge of the Puna mission chapel, Star of the Sea, which became another attractive "Painted Church" thanks to the art work of Father Evarist Gielen who came to Puna in 1927.

Overexertion on his difficult travels finally overtook the valiant Father Pouzot after thirty years of devoted labor, and he had to withdraw for six months of rest and recovery at Honolulu, returning in February 1879. He kept on faithfully for another ten years, when Father Maxime Andre was sent to his aid. Pouzot died on April 30, 1895, after fifty years of faithful service in Hilo.

After forty-six years of service, the twin-towered Saint Joseph's Church required extensive repairs in 1906. It was the brilliant work of Father James C. Beissel, who came to Hilo in 1909, that made the church "one of the most flourishing centers of Catholic life in Hawai'i." His great physical accomplishment was building the present, beautiful Saint Joseph's and the new large rectory completed in 1919.

22
"UNCLE GEORGE" LYCURGUS ENTERTAINS

George Lycurgus
Hawai'i State Archives

Pele has been and still is the most famous attraction of the Big Island. Pilgrims from everywhere have come to see the wonders of Hawai'i's great volcano.

Greeting world notables coming to behold the startling sights of Pele's displays was the affable host of Volcano House, George Lycurgus, fondly known as "Uncle George." Born in 1859 in Sparta, he served in the Greek Army, operated an oyster grotto in San Francisco, and in 1889 joined a brother and cousin in the fruit business in Honolulu. Gregarious George was soon socializing with "sugar king" Claus Spreckles, King

Kalākaua, and Queen Liliʻuokalani, and entertaining Robert Louis Stevenson at his Hotel Sans Souci at Waikīkī. He also owned the Union Grill in Honolulu.

An 1894 horseback trip to the volcano, over the new road opened from Hilo, persuaded him that this would become a prime tourist attraction and brought him to Hilo in 1902 to operate the Demosthenes Cafe, which later became the Lycurgus Building. It was 1904 when George bought the Volcano House and in 1908 he added to his tourist resting places the Hilo Hotel, where friend Kalākaua had formerly enjoyed relaxing and playing cards. An untimely trip to Greece in 1914 left him caught there by World War I until 1920.

The first Volcano House at Kīlauea Crater opened in 1861. *Lyman House Memorial Museum*

His stock in the Volcano House went to the Inter Island Steam Navigation Company, which spent one hundred fifty thousand dollars to remodel and expand the hotel. Fate brought it back to George for just three hundred dollars at an auction in 1933, when the company went bankrupt during the Depression.

After a fire in 1940, he rebuilt the hotel and continued ruling there as entertainer of important visitors until his death in 1960 at age one hundred and one. He courted goddess Pele with donations of gin, winning some spectacular eruptions to bug-eye his guests. Princes from Europe, presidents, and popular sport and entertainment figures enjoyed the big shows with George and played cribbage with him, leaving behind a museum of autographed photos.

CHRONOLOGICAL LIST OF EVENTS

750 ca		Marquesans land in Hawai'i
1000 ca		Pā'ao comes to Hawai'i from Samoa
1200 ca		Tahitians come to Hawai'i
1550 ca		Building of Hale-O-Keawe
1775 ca		Kamehameha's birth
1778		Cook's first landing in Hawai'i
1779	January 17	Cook's ships at Kealakekua Bay
	February 14	Cook's death
1790		Isaac Davis and John Young in Hawai'i
1791		Kamehameha repels Maui invasion
1792–1794		Vancouver brings cattle
1794	February 25	Kamehameha cedes Hawai'i Island to Great Britain
1795		Kamehameha conquers Maui and O'ahu
1803		Richard Cleveland brings first horses
1808		'Ōpūkaha'ia sails to America as Henry Obookiah
1809		John Palmer Parker lands on Hawai'i
1810		Isaac Davis dies
1812		Kamehameha retires to Kona
1815		John Parker returns to Hawai'i from the Orient
1818	February 17	'Ōpūkaha'ia dies at Cornwall, Connecticut
1819	May 8	Kamehameha dies at Kailua
	August	Kalanimōkū receives Catholic baptism aboard *L'Uranie*
	October 23	*Thaddeus* sails from Boston
1820–1844		Kuakini governor of Hawai'i
1820	April 4	*Thaddeus* at Kailua
1823	June 24–September 3	Missionaries explore island
	December 10	First church in Kailua finished

1824	January		Joseph Goodrich and Samuel Ruggles start Hilo Mission
	March 29		Church at Kaʻawaloa dedicated
	July		Kamehameha II dies in London
	December 22		Kapiʻolani defies Pele at Volcano
1826	February		Second Kailua church started
1828	February 21		Elizabeth Bishop dies
	December 1		Artemas Bishop marries Delia Stone
1830	October 15		Hilo church dedicated
1832			David Lyman in Hilo; Dwight Baldwin and Lorenzo Lyons in Waimea
1834	July		David Douglas is killed in bull pit
1835			Titus Coan in Hilo
	December 1		Kailua Church destroyed by fire
	December 1		John Young dies
1836	January 1		Present Mokuʻaikaua Church in Kailua started; Hilo Boarding School for Boys started
1837	February 4		Mokuʻaikaua Church dedication
	May 14		Betsey Lyons dies at Honolulu Abner Wilcox at Hilo
1838	July 14		Lorenzo Lyons marries Lucia Smith at Hilo
1839			Building of stone church at Kaʻawaloa
1840	June 26		Fathers Robert Walsh and Louis Heurtel in Kona
1841	May		Kapiʻolani dies; Elias Bond in Kohala; John Paris starts Waiʻōhinu Mission
1842			Father Joachim Marechal in Kaʻū
1844			Kuakini dies
1846			Father Charles Pouzot in Hilo
1847	February 18		Mary Grant Paris dies in Hilo
1849			Charles Wetmore in Hilo
1852			John Paris returns to take over Kaʻawaloa Mission

1855–1869		Ruth Ke'elikōlani becomes governor of Hawai'i
1855		Saint Michael's Church dedication in Kailua
	October 11	Kalāhikiola Churchat dedication in Kohala
1857		'Imiola Church dedication in Waimea
1859	April 8	Haili Church dedication in Hilo
	April 21	Joachim Marechal dies in Kailua
1861		Thurstons leaves Kailua Mission
1863	February 14	Kohala Sugar Company organization
1868	March 11	Asa Thurston dies in Honolulu
	March 25	John Palmer Parker dies
1868		Year of destructive earthquakes
1874	December 3	Kohala Girls' School opens
1876	October 13	Lucy Thurston dies at Honolulu
1879	July	Wetmore sets up first telephone line on island
1881	May 12	Ellen Bond dies at Kohala
1883	May 24	Ruth Ke'elikōlani dies
	July 23	Lucy Wetmore dies
1884	October 4	David Lyman dies in Hilo
	December 5	Sarah Lyman dies in Hilo
1886	October 6	Lorenzo Lyons dies in Waimea
1892	April 27	Lucia Smith Lyons dies in Waimea
1895	April 30	Father Louis Pouzot dies in Hilo
1896	July 24	Elias Bond dies in Kohala
1898	February 8	Charles Wetmore dies in Hilo
1902		Saint Benedict's Church dedication in Kona
1904		George Lycurgus buys Volcano House
1940		Volcano House is rebuilt after fire

SUGGESTED READING

Alexander, Mary Charlotte, *Dr. Baldwin of Lahaina*, Stanford, 1953.

Brennan, Joseph, *The Parker Ranch of Hawai'i*, New York, 1979.

Daws, Gavan, *Shoal of Time*, Honolulu, 1974.

Coan, Titus, *Life in Hawai'i*, New York, 1882.

Damon, Ethel M., *Father Bond of Kohala*, Honolulu, 1927.

Doyle, Emma Lyons, *Makua Laiana*, Honolulu, 1953.

Dwight, Edwin, *Memoirs of Henry Obookiah*, Kingsport, Tenn., 1968.

Ellis, William, *Journal of William Ellis*, Honolulu, 1963.

Greenwell, Alice, *The House of Young*, Smithtown, New York, 1982.

Loomis, Albertine, *Grapes of Canaan: Hawai'i 1820*, Honolulu, 1972.

Lyman, Henry M., *Hawaiian Yesterdays*, Chicago, 1906.

Martin, Margaret Greet, *The Lymans of Hilo*, Hilo, 1979.

Olson, Gunder E., *The Story of the Volcano House*, Hilo, 1984.

Piercy, LaRue W., *Hawai'i Truth Stranger Than Fiction*, Honolulu, 1987.

Schoofs, Robert, *Pioneers of the Faith*, Honolulu, 1978.

Thurston, Lucy G., *Life and Times*, Honolulu, 1934.

Zambucka, Kristin, *The High Chiefess Ruth Keelikolani*, Honolulu, 1977.

ABOUT THE AUTHOR

LaRue W. Piercy was a graduate of high school at Binghamton, New York (his birthplace), and of Western Reserve University, Cleveland, Ohio, where he earned his M.A. in English in 1931. He taught at Emerson Junior High School, Lakewood, Ohio, and then at Western Reserve Academy, Hudson, Ohio, from 1929 to 1941. His work in school journalism won him the presidency of both the Cleveland and Ohio journalism associations, and national recognition. He reported school news to city papers and established the academy alumni association.

During World War II, he served as a personnel counselor at the Glenn L. Martin Company, Middle River, Maryland, returning to his home in Hudson in 1944. There for two years he edited the weekly *Hudson Times* and did everything necessary for getting it published and delivered. He also published community directories to obtain a record of people in the towns served by the Times.

From that experience he joined the Mullin Kille Company of Chilicothe, Ohio, and supervised city directory canvasses from 1947 to 1951. Then, after two years as assistant manager of Rural Directories, Bowling Green, Ohio, he returned to Mullin Kille to serve as chief canvass manager until 1965, and after that doing compilation work at his home in Hawai'i until 1974. His directory work took him to twenty-one different states, the largest directory being that of Phoenix, Arizona, in 1950 and 1951.

The Piercys first visited Hawai'i in l956 when on a Pacific circle tour, they then bought land on Hawai'i Island in 1961 while on a round-the-world tour. They also traveled the Pacific, Asia, and Europe widely. Their first travel abroad was in 1932 on a bicycle tour of Hungary, as Mrs. Piercy was a native of Magyar.

Other Mutual titles by LaRue W. Piercy include—*Hawai'i This and That, Hawai'i's Missionary Saga,* and *Hawai'i Truth Stranger Than Fiction.*

OTHER BIG ISLAND HISTORY BOOKS FROM MUTUAL PUBLISHING

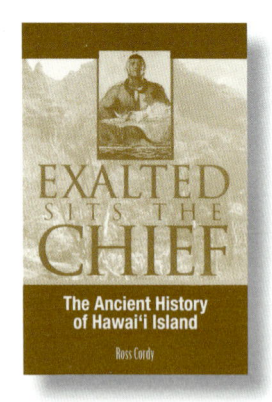

Exalted Sits the Chief: The Ancient History of Hawai'i Island
By Ross Cordy

"Exalted Sits the Chief is one of the most important books ever published in the field of Hawaiian archeology and history. It is the first book-length effort to combine the rich traditional history and ethnography of the Big Island with the vast amount of archeological data accumulated over the last 50 years." Dr. David Tuggle—International Archeological Research Institute.

6 in. x 9 in. • 472 pp
Softcover
ISBN-10: 1-56647-340-3
ISBN-13: 978-1-56647-340-8
$19.95
Hardcover
ISBN-10: 1-56647-341-1
ISBN-13: 978-1-56647-341-5
$24.95

Hawai'i's Missionary Saga
By LaRue W. Piercy

The amazing story of the trials and tribulations of the men and women who helped bring Christianity to the islands of Hawai'i. Detailed appendices and an index provide a wealth of information about this fascinating saga.

6 in. x 9 in. • 232 pp
Softcover
ISBN-10: 0-935180-05-2
ISBN-13: 978-0-935180-05-3
$16.95

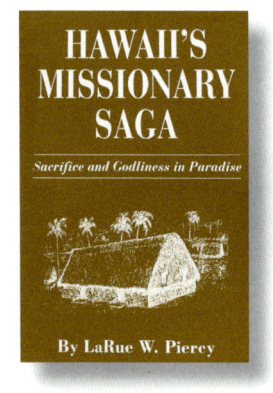

Ancient Sites of Hawai'i
By Van James

This informative and easy-to-follow guidebook makes the ancient sites of the Big Island of Hawai'i reachable to the general public for the first time. Grouping the sites by location, *Ancient Sites of Hawai'i* characterizes the cultural background of five main types of sites: heiau (temples), pōhaku (sacred stones), petroglyphs, caves, and fishponds.

6 in. x 9 in. • 176 pp
Softcover
ISBN-10: 1-56647-200-8
ISBN-13: 978-1-56647-200-5
$13.95

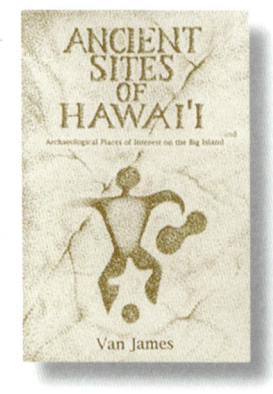

To order please visit our website:
www.mutualpublishing.com
or email us at info@mutualpublishing.com